The Art of

Self-Leadership

Arthur L. Andrews

ACKNOWLEDGEMENTS

To Debbie: my wife, advisor, and my best friend. Thank you for being the wind beneath my wings. You are my queen and I love you!

To my children, Rashime and Ayana, I am proud to be your Dad. You are the apples of my eye and I love you so much!

I dedicate this book to the memory of my father and mother, Clarence and Mary Andrews.

To Elder Convey and Thelma Thorpe, my second set of parents. They are the ones who raised me and gave me my core values. To my third set of parents, Dr. Claude and Jocelyn Thomas, who endured my turbulent teens and provided me with a positive and consistent example. I will always love you! Jesse Phillips (POP), you have been the best father-in-law a man can ever have, thank you and I Love You.

To all the members of my family who consistently supported me through the years, I say, "Thank you so much!"

I acknowledge Les Brown who inspired me to get on the path.

I acknowledge Marcia Snow who was so instrumental in getting me out there. Thanks to Dr. Ed and Sandra Montgomery for all your love and support. Thanks to Travis Rucker for providing a platform. I will never forget you man. I appreciate Mark Taylor and Craig Harris for looking out for a brother. Thanks to Walter Ballard for coaching me and telling me what I needed to hear and not what I wanted to hear. I acknowledge Dr. Bobby Jones for taking a chance on an unknown and Janice Brown for consistent encouragement through the years. To Drs. I.V. and Bridgette Hilliard for inviting me into your home and sharing powerful, positive principles for success and prosperity, I say thanks. I will never, ever forget the experience. I give a special thanks to Dr. Benjamin Reeves for tremendous exposure. Evelyn Patterson, you are such a blessing (in the spirit of Jabez!!). Elder T. Marshall Kelly, words cannot encompass the symbolism of what an inspiration you are to me.

I extend many thanks to the Big Speak Speakers Bureau for keeping me on the road, and to Henry, Jeanette, Marissa, and Victoria Pineda for demonstrating what true love is. I love you all so much! Henry, thank you for being there when I needed you the most. Jeff and Morgan Long, thank you. Pastor and Sis. Leroy Woodard: thank you for the encouragement and seeds that were sown.

I extend the warmest acknowledgements to all of the event planners, producers, and promoters that have contributed to my life and professional growth. Thank you so much. To the hundreds of thousands that have attended my seminars and speeches throughout the world, thank you for all your support.

Thank you Jeff Yentzer for all that you've done.

Angela Jaynes, what can I say, you're an angel! Thanks for all your assistance, patience, dedication and creativeness in helping make this book happen.

FOREWARD
By J. Maxim Fields

For over a decade my telephone has been ringing. And when I answer it I am greeted with a joyous, "Good morning! The mark of greatness is upon you!"

Arthur L. Andrews is the human version of a double-cappuccino. He is electrifying and truly bigger than life.

I first met this extraordinary human being when he came to speak to a group of young (and not so young) people in Los Angeles. After the meeting I asked him to speak to our students at the Perecon Institute (*personal finance*—www.maximfields.com).

The Institute teaches individuals and family units the exact science of saving money, living with wise debt, and making wise financial investments. For over an entire year Arthur would fly out and energize the audiences wherever he spoke. I learned that it is not what a man says on stage that really counts. It is what he says in the quiet moments when there is no crowd.

His impact is immeasurable. Ten years later people are still asking about Arthur L. Andrews. Here is all that I know: the man lives what he teaches. In this day and age that quality is truly rare.

I urge you to take this book; ingest it. Seek to understand its principles. Live them. Then teach them to your future generations. And may God bless all the works of your hands.

INTRODUCTION

Thank you for picking up this book! It tells me something about you. You are still searching and that's a good thing! You're a person who refuses to live beneath your privilege. You are someone who wants to develop your talents and gifts more fully. No one on this planet can bring what you bring. There's no one quite like you. Your uniqueness shines through everything you do. Your talents, your abilities, your knowledge, your skills are unprecedented. It is both a challenging and exciting time to be alive. Never, ever has there been a time like this in history. There is an explosion of limitless possibilities.

The principles set forth in this book are not superficial, but powerful! Here you will find precious truths that will inevitably blast you out of your own personal rut of mediocrity. This success system is designed for those who are willing to commit to consistency and to journal their progress daily. This is not a complicated system. It requires a minimal amount of time each day. There is nothing strenuous about it. I will be your personal success coach guiding you through each step. I will tell you specifically what to do to create tremendous momentum in your life.

Does this system work? It will work if you work it. Here's my experience: In the beginning of the nineties I was broke and frustrated, working at a job doing just enough not to get fired, paid enough not to quit. I was hanging in there for the dental plan, and that's not an ideal way to live. In the wise words of Henry David Thoreau, there are unfortunately so many people "living lives of quiet desperation."

I was one of them until I tapped into this knowledge that has transformed my thinking and dramatically improved my level of confidence. Knowledge is the foundation of our future; it provides you with the ability to live above fear. Increased knowledge gives you a clear vision. Helen Keller said, "The most pathetic person in the world is the one who has sight, but no vision."

What is your vision of the future? How do you see it developing, regardless of what the critics think or say? There's a story I love about a little boy who was painting with a brand new watercolor set. His mother inquired as to what he was about to paint and the boy answered, "I'm painting God." The mother, endeavoring to coach her son in the development of this piece responded with, "Now son, no one knows what God looks like." The boy creatively and confidently continued to move his brush on the large piece of construction paper and replied, "They will when I'm finished!"

Knowing what you want and where you are going is the stuff vision is made of. Robert Collier said it best: **"See things as you would have them be instead of as they are."**

Thomas Edison once said, "If you were to do all that you are capable of doing you would astonish yourself!" You must have a strong desire to succeed if you wish to play a key role in the 21st Century. I encourage you to never, never, <u>never</u>, give up! Remember – it wasn't raining when Noah built the ark!

You may find that you are already immersed in a process of ongoing personal development and implementing many of the exercises and techniques described in this book. That's great! You will accelerate the results.

You may find that you are overwhelmed by all the things

you have to do from day to day and don't feel you will be able to commit to all the steps that are required in this system.

Keep calm. Remember, masterpieces take time. Don't endeavor to do everything at once, no matter how zealous you may be. Simply precede one step at a time. Each concept, each idea, each step sown into your subconscious mind conscientiously and consistently taken, will produce a rich harvest. As Napoleon Hill said, "Whatever the mind can conceive and believe it can achieve."

HOW TO USE THIS BOOK

1. Read the book from cover to cover without doing any of the exercises.

2. Start doing the exercises in the order and pace suggested.

3. Reread the book slowly and thoughtfully, high-lighting the passages that impress you the most.

4. Understand and complete each Action Point. When you see [Action Point] there is something required on your part.

5. Tell a friend about Arthur (www.ArthurAndrews.com)

Table of Contents

Chapter 1

The Power Of Happiness

The Power of Happiness

Are you happy? Think about it. Are you really happy? When I ask this question I usually get a blank stare. Sometimes I get that glazed-over look. You know, the one you're displaying right now. Don't get upset. I'm just kidding. Stay loose!

One day while shopping in a fine department store I asked one of the sales professionals this question and the response was, "What do you mean? It all depends on what you're talking about." I didn't think this was a very complicated question, rather a very simple one. Either "Yes, I'm happy" or "No, I'm not happy."

I've discovered that this thing we call happiness has a lot to do with life matching our expectations of how things ought to be, and when they don't, in creep those feelings of depression, lethargy, and frustration. Blaming others (parents, bosses, corporations, Amway, immigrants, fate, weather, bad luck, the government, or the horoscope) is just a waste of your creative energy. The real issue is: What are we doing about our own unhappiness?

In life you're the fly or the windshield, the thermometer or the thermostat. You're either in the way or on the way. Life is about choices. Will you move on with your life or will you remain chained to your past?

When I was a little boy it was part of my Aunt Thelma's mission statement that each year she would take me to see the Ringling Brothers Barnum and Bailey Circus in Madison Square Garden. My favorite act was the elephants. As I reminisce there's something very interesting that comes to mind.

These large animals were tied to a stake by a very thin piece of rope. Now the elephants, being as massive as they are, had the power to pull the stake out of the ground, snap that rope in half and go anywhere they wanted to. The question then becomes why didn't they? Because when these elephants were very young they were restrained by the very same ropes and held down by the very same stakes.

They struggled and struggled with all of their might until they finally gave up. They could not pull the stake out. They could not break the rope. Having learned the lesson well, the elephants accepted the fact that they cannot escape.

It is a fact that when the elephant was very young it couldn't pull up the stake, but why is it that now that it is full grown it won't just pull this stake out the ground and walk away? The massive animal is not restrained by the rope but tied to a belief about the rope. The elephant is restricted by its own belief system. In its mind it believes that it can't break free, so it remains and doesn't even make an effort to escape. What a lesson!

Your history is not your destiny. You do not have to stay tied to the limitations that others have set for you. There is always, always, a way of escape. You are not a victim. You are powerful!

Emmett Fox said, "Do it trembling if you must, but do it." What's stopping you? Are you tied to a negative experience of the past that has you in a vice? Popular gospel singer Vickie Winans has a song on one of her CDs that says, "Shake Yourself Loose!" I love it because it is so liberating! That's what I did. I shook the people, circumstances, and things from my life that I believed were contributing to my unhappiness.

It takes courage and discipline to get freed and to remain free. Each of us has a decision to make about our happiness. We all go through stuff. Your experience is not that unique. What's the worst thing that could happen? And if it did, would you still be alive?

Could it be that you just might be taking things a little too seriously? Remember: arrive at your decisions in life by choice, never pressure.

Abraham Lincoln said, "Most people are about as happy as they make up their mind to be." Happiness is a decision. It is a state of being, a state of mind.

What do you really want? I think this is a good place to start. This system is designed to enable you to get what you really want. This system, I repeat, will assist you in getting anything that is within legal limits of human attainment.

However, there are a few prerequisites: You must first demand more from yourself. Secondly, you must be willing to transform your thinking. And thirdly, you must be willing to pay the required price. Remember: There's always free cheese in a mousetrap! The universal law says that you don't get something for nothing.

This can be the greatest moment of your life! This is the most powerful place you can be. Most tombstones read, "Woulda, shoulda, coulda." Some read, "Here lies_____. He/she was going to be happy." Some will read, "I knew this was going to happen!" One lady's read, "I told them I was sick!" I'm not being morbid; I'm just making a point. There is a poem I love that goes like this:

> There once was a very cautious man who
> never laughed or cried,
> he never risked, he never tried.
> And when one day he passed away
> his insurance was denied.
> For since he never lived,
> they claimed he never died.
> Of all the saddest words of tongue and pen
> the saddest of them all is what could have
> been.

In the movie "Out of Africa," Karen Blixen said, "My greatest fear is that I would come to the end of my life and suddenly realize that I have lived someone else's dream."

Whose dream are you committed to? If you don't have a plan for your life, someone else does. If you don't work for your goals you will work for someone else's.

Is time passing you by? Years ago, I was shopping in a mall and stopped by one of those electronic stores. I noticed a clock counting down the years you have left on the planet, according to your age. It was amazing and at the same time frightening, especially if it appeared that your time was up.

Arthur L. Andrews

Talk about fear factor!

Benjamin Franklin once wrote, "Most people die at the age of 25 and don't get buried until they're 75." Most people slip along from youth to old age with an eerie feeling that they missed out on something, but never come to the realization of what that something is.

Ponder these words given to us by the famous author anonymous: "First I was dying to finish high school and start college. And then I was dying to finish college and start working. And then I was dying to marry and have children. And then I was dying for my children to grow old enough for school so I could return to work. And then I was dying to retire. And now I am dying ... and suddenly I realize I forgot to live."

In Dr. Bernie Segal's book entitled "Miracles" he wrote, "One of the most common precursors of cancer is a feeling of emptiness." In other words, having no central purpose can make you physically sick as well as cater to your unhappiness.

To quote John Gardner, "Human beings have always employed an enormous amount of clever devices for running away from themselves. We can keep ourselves so busy, fill our lives with so many diversions, stuff our heads with so much knowledge, involve ourselves with so many people, and cover so much ground, that we never have the time to probe the fearful and wonderful world within. By middle life, most of us are accomplished fugitives from ourselves."

There are people all around us who appear to be happy and successful, but in reality are living in pain and misery. They smile for the cameras and look great at social functions, but leave with lonely, empty feelings. Many of their marriages end in divorce, filled with pain and heartache. They nip and tuck, but still they long for inner peace. They have mega-bank accounts, but have no idea who their real friends are. They may even grace platforms and endeavor to give you prescriptions for happiness, and yet they fail to benefit from their own advice.

Many years ago William Marsten conducted a two-year survey where he asked over three thousand people this soul-piercing question: "Why did you show up on the planet?" An overwhelming ninety-four percent said they didn't have a clue. They were waiting for something to happen. Perhaps they were waiting for Publisher's Clearing House, the lottery, or someone to come rescue them and inevitably bring with them happiness. Stop waiting and take responsibility for your life!

What do you really want out of life? What will it take to become the person you desire to be? What would you accomplish if you knew you could not fail? I believe that lack of focus, purpose, and discipline are the root causes of failure and misery.

If you don't have a clear, definite purpose, you lack the focus desperately needed to achieve your major objectives in life. One of the reasons most people feel stuck is because they know that they are more than what they have been demonstrating. Are you much more than you've been demonstrating? If the answer is yes, then why aren't you demonstrating more? Is it fear? What's stopping you?

Lawrence is unhappy with his current position. He doesn't know what he really wants but he's pretty confident he doesn't have it yet. He constantly criticizes and quarrels with his manager and co-workers, so he is always passed up for any type of raise or promotion. He likes to play the victim role. He will share his story with anyone who is willing to listen, so his circle of friends has grown smaller. Lawrence is very bitter and believes that life's unfair. He proclaims, "You can't win for losing! That's life!!"

Wrong Lawrence, that's your life! Unfortunately, Lawrence will continue to experience the same results until he becomes an active participant in his own rescue. Lawrence may be like so many others who are not willing to face the truth about themselves. To discover that the key reason they are where they are today (and with whom they are in relationship with) is because at some point in their lives they made a conscious choice to be there. This can be alarming.

What should be even more alarming is to pretend to have a plan for your happiness. Most people have noble intentions, but fail to follow through.

Karen constantly whined and complained about how unhappy she was with her weight, and how it was preventing her from being in a loving, meaningful, and satisfying relationship. She insisted that she wanted to change that, and she was willing to do whatever it would take to resolve the issue. Her friend Shirley suggested that she make an investment of one thousand dollars and become a member of one of the most prestigious health clubs in the city. Karen loved the club and how this new program would benefit her health and wellness, but she soon became intimidated by some of the other females who were fit and trim. She only visited the club about six times and quit.

Comparing yourself to others is the doorway to insanity. We are who we are and any desire to look like another or be better than another is created by our own insecurities. Work at your own pace.

When will it happen? When it happens. How long will it take? As long as it takes. What if you don't achieve all the results? You've enjoyed the trip.

Power Method:

Action Plan

Make a list of ten things that you really, really want. Don't immediately start jotting things down. I want you to pause and think about it for a moment. We don't want history to repeat itself, so please take your time and decide what's truly right for you.

Warning: This list should be for your eyes only! It has been said, "If you don't want people to rain on your parade don't let them know what street it's coming down." Embrace the power of secrecy!

Here are a few suggestions that I believe will assist you in developing your list:

1. Be specific. Avoid generalities such as "more money." Instead state: "I now earn an income of $_____ a year."

2. Look to see if there is a conflict in your desires. It would be quite challenging for

Shaquille O'Neal to put on his list "World-Class Jockey!" Think over this point and resolve any inconsistencies that may be on your list.

3. Don't list things in which you have only a casual interest. List things that you have a burning desire for, that just the thought of them gets you juiced. Do that which brings life, not that which deadens your spirit.

4. Know that inspiration without adequate preparation is the beginning of delusion. For example, before running for mayor of your city make sure you have thorough knowledge of political science. Likewise, it is foolish to expect to practice medicine without a thorough knowledge of the sciences. Before you take on the responsibility of supporting a wife and children make sure you can support yourself. If you want to go in business for yourself, create a business plan. If you fail to plan, you plan to fail!

5. Don't list things that belong to others. Seek a husband or a wife by all means, but not someone else's. Never list or frame your desire in a way that involves injury or deprivation. Attempts to injure or treat people unjustly can and will backfire on you in an

unexpected and painful manner. What goes around comes around! Any worthwhile goal can be achieved without hurting other people.

6. Frame each desire in a positive and constructive way, clearly declare the thing or condition that you seek, and refuse to discuss anything that you wish to discard or eliminate from your life.

    For example, don't write, "I want to get these negative people out of my life." It's a worthy aspiration, but poorly expressed. Every time you write, speak, or think about these negative people you reaffirm the fact that they are in your life. Write instead, "I now develop powerful, positive relationships with people of honor and integrity."

Note that the phrase "I develop" is stronger and more constructive than "I want…" or "I need…" or "I wish…" or "I would like…." Instead fashion your desire with words that express that it is now accomplished. "It is done!" The Book of Wisdom says, "Now faith is the substance of things hoped for, and the evidence of things not seen!" (Hebrews 11:1) Call those things that be not, as though they were! You can change your life through faith!

The Art of Self-Leadership

Here are a few more examples you can use to assist yourself in your quest to break free:

Don't write, "I want to stop overeating," or "I want to stop smoking," or "I want to conquer my shyness," or "I want to get out of debt," and/or "I want to get out of this depressing environment." These statements reaffirm overeating, smoking, shyness, debt, and a depressing environment.

The subconscious mind cannot differentiate between what is imaginary and what is real. It just gathers data. Whatever it receives, it records. (I will explain more about the subconscious mind in Chapter 2.) There is no point in having your subconscious work against you. Say or write things that are consistent with what you really want to have and where you really want to go in life.

Enlist your subconscious as an ally. Write the following: "I now develop positive habits of self-control. I am poised, powerful, and confident at all times. I now move into a peaceful, pleasant, and stimulating environment."

I want you to spend an average of fifteen minutes a day affirming your desires constructively and watch these desires become a concrete reality for you.

7. Now, I want you to rearrange your list of the ten things you want in order of priority. This

will help you find the item that you will work on first. Begin with something easy, something that you know is within your reach.

Remember, you crawl before you walk, then you run! If you want to learn to play the piano wouldn't it be easier to start single notes slowly before advancing to rapid chord progressions? If you desire to be a carpenter, wouldn't it be a whole lot easier to learn to drive nails before taking on the construction of a house? So it is with your list. Begin with the easiest project. Success and completion in it will encourage you to develop more skills and confidence for the next project or subsequent items on your master dream list.

When there's clarity we approach life differently. Be more focused and confident about the future. If you have any questions with regard to the placement of items on your "Master Dream List," here are a few suggestions that can assist you:

A) Ask yourself, "Which of these items can I achieve quickly?"
Reduce my weight by fifteen pounds

Learn another language.

Develop a more positive, pleasant attitude toward my manager and co-workers.

Apply the test of time. Learning another language from scratch can take several months. Losing fifteen pounds with proper coaching and disciplined effort could be accomplished in two to three months. A change in attitude toward my manager and co-workers can be accomplished the very next workday.

Okay, so your list would be in the following order:

- Develop a more positive and pleasant attitude toward my manager and co-workers.
- Reduce my weight by fifteen pounds.
- Learn another language.

B) Another suggestion: Now ask yourself, "Which of these items can be accomplished with the knowledge and abilities I now possess? Which of them will require new knowledge or the cultivation of new skills?"

C) After careful thought, and application of the first two suggestions, you may find that two items seem equally easy. Now ask yourself, "Which of the two is more important to me?" Put that one above the other. Another way of framing the question is, "If I could have only one of the two which one would it be?" That one is the most important and should be placed above the other.

Action Plan

Take the items on your Master Dream List and tabulate them in order of priority, the easiest at the top.

That required more thought, and I am proud of you! Great job! You are now already far ahead of most people: You know what you want, and in and of itself that creates happiness. In addition you have developed a plan to accomplish it!

Your Master Dream List will be the basis for this on-going process of personal as well as professional development. You will refer to it often. You will find that, as you make progress, you will want to revise it from time to time. It's all right to make changes; it's a part of life.

You are a creative, dynamic, evolving full expression of life. In one month's time you will be somewhat different from what you are today. In a year's time you will be noticeably different.

Allen Cohen says, "Creating a life is like forming a vase on a potter's wheel. We start out with an amorphous chunk of material and we continually mold and remold it. The clay goes through many revolutions; each time it passes through your hands you have another opportunity to bring your work of art closer to life. No great artist forms his masterpiece on the first attempt. The hands are constantly pushing, pressing, releasing, and refining. Art, like life, is a process of continuous revising, updating, and improving."

Remember: Don't tell other people what's on your list. Don't even mention what you're doing! This is very, very important.

Happiness is living on purpose!

Arthur L. Andrews

MASTER DREAM LIST

The Art of Self-Leadership

Summary
Chapter 1

Remember, masterpieces take time!

You are not a victim; you are powerful!

It will work, if you work it!

Ask yourself what you really want!

Make a list of the things you want!

Be specific about what it is that you want!

Be realistic about what you want!

Don't injure or deprive others in the process of getting what you want!

Forget the past!

Positively affirm what you want for an average of fifteen minutes a day!

Prioritize your list in order of ease—easiest first!

Confidence grows with completion!

Keep your plans strictly to yourself!

Chapter 2

The Power
Of
Thought

The Power of Thought

Mark Twain had it right when he said, "Life does not consist mainly, or even largely, of facts and happenings. It consists mainly of the storm of the thought that is forever flowing through one's head."

In order to create tremendous momentum in your life you must retrain your brain. In other words you must get it to operate the way you want it to, so that it will do what you want it to do consistently. You've read books like this, attended seminars that promise to make you rich, and listened to audio programs that guarantee phenomenal results.

The ideas and concepts were interesting, but there was still a feeling of emptiness. By now you probably know all of the "how to" you'll ever need. You know *how to* lose weight, and *how to* win friends and influence people. You know *how to* develop a more positive attitude, *how to* make more money, and *how to* have a more happy and successful marriage. And the list goes on. You see—the challenge is not knowing but getting yourself to take consistent action toward the desired result.

The gurgling and cooing of a baby are noise but not speech. The baby must learn to control those noises and shape them into words if its going to have its needs met down the road. It is the same with thought; most people believe they are thinking, when in reality they are only daydreaming. Thinking is a controlled, directed mental process. It can be learned. It can be practiced. It can be taught. Why is it so important to think effectively? Because everything begins with a thought. When you think about winning, guess what? When you think about losing, guess what?

An unhappy thought makes your life unhappy. I asked a guy one day how he was doing and he looked at me with a scowl saying, "I'm fine!!!" I immediately replied, "Then please notify your face!" I am convinced of this one basic truth: that whatever is on the inside will show up on the outside. This is something that most people think they are hiding. Unhappy thoughts create an unhappy countenance. Sick thoughts make you look and feel sick. Fearful, doubtful thoughts create failure and keep you broke emotionally as well as financially. Henry Ford shared these words of wisdom,

"Think you can, think you can't, either way you'll be right."

What do you believe has stopped you from creating the outstanding life you've imagined for yourself? If you are not there, then where are you? Do you think maybe it's time now to take a different route in the area of your thinking?

I'd like to share a story about a traveler who was driving down an interstate on his way to a major city and accidentally got off at the wrong exit. After passing through a small community, he pulled up to a local convenience store to get something to snack on and some gas to continue his journey. As he approached the counter to pay the traveler said, "I need your help. I'm lost."

The cashier smiled and asked, "Do you know where you are?"

"I believe I do; I saw the name of the town a few miles back," answered the traveler.

"Do you know where you want to go?" asked the cashier.

"Yes," the traveler replied, and named his destination.

Handing him the receipt the cashier said, "You're

not lost young man; you just need some directions." The cashier then proceeded to show the traveler how to get back to the main interstate.

There are many people who are like the traveler in that story. They feel lost. They are what Zig Ziglar refers to as "wandering generalities, rather than meaningful specifics." They need some directions. They're here, they're there, and they're everywhere. They have no road map. They are just trying different interstates, hoping they'll reach their destination somehow. The Book of Life says, "A double minded person is unstable in all their ways" (James 1:7-8).

Indecisiveness can impede your growth. Not making a decision means you have already made your decision. Decision is the key. You must get to a point in your life where you say to yourself: "I've got to do this! I may have to do it trembling, but I'm going to do this!" This is a time when you may cry, or may even want to give up. You may feel lonely and/or lost. Remember you're not lost; you just need some directions. That's why I showed up. Remember, nothing just happens by chance. There is always a purpose. There is always a plan. I am in your life by design. Just how far you go in life will depend largely on how far you are willing to go in regard to your thinking. The greatest challenge you will face is taking the first step in the right direction. I know you have had challenging times and life has seemed so unfair. Maybe you're at a point where you're saying, "What's the use?" "I've heard this all before." "This is a waste of time." "Here we go again." With a thought pattern like this it gets harder and harder to take the first step.

Are you ready to take the first step? Let's begin with a basic truth: "Nothing and no one can make you look or feel inferior without your consent." Decide right now that you will only give your energy to those things, circumstances, and people that turn your power up, not down. The reason why this is so important is because your subconscious is being programmed daily.

Corporations pay millions of dollars to come up with ways of entering your subconscious mind for profit. Many of us don't realize that we have been programmed for years to behave the way we do. How many times have you wondered why it is so hard to go after what you really want and enjoy the first-class lifestyle you so rightly deserve? Because you have been programmed—pure and simple!

Your pattern of thinking can be traced back to your childhood. We started out as emotional sponges, soaking up every experience, whether it was negative or positive. We all learned to be winners or losers. It is not a part of our biological makeup; it's just our learning styles that were transmitted by our parent(s) or care giver(s).

My wife and I have witnessed first hand that what is seen and heard in the behaviors of a parent has a huge impact on a child. One father shared a rather interesting story with me. He told me of his then-four-year young daughter who became the main attraction. She began to blow an unusually large number of bubbles from a wand. The children and parents grew quite amused with his little girl. On her fourth attempt, she blew through the device only to see one big bubble come out of the hole in the wand and burst. She immediately looked at the wand, and elevated her little voice and said: "What the #%@ *!!!"

Her parents understandably became somewhat embarrassed. But what is the major teaching point in all of this? The little girl had incorporated every-thing she had observed her parents do and say up to this point in her young life, and it had unfortunately become her model for handling conflict and meet-ing life's challenges. The little girl had become a garden and was only producing what had been planted.

To understand this more fully we need to under-stand how the mind processes information. We have a conscious and subconscious mind. Our conscious mind acts like a security guard; it inspects information to see whether it is appropriate to enter or not. Once we determine how this information is to be interpreted, it then passes through to the subconscious part of us. Now, on the other hand, the subconscious mind doesn't make judgments. It is like a computer: give it a command and it will perform accordingly.

If you hit delete, it will delete; hit save, and it will save. It's waiting for you to tell it what to do and how to perform.

When we were children we were totally innocent and received our information from forces outside ourselves. We were not programming but being programmed. We collected the behavior patterns of our parent(s) or caregiver(s) and put them in little emotional suitcases and carried them around with us.

Many of us today are unfortunately still dragging this baggage around. Most of our parents were only doing to us what their parents did to them. Most of them were not aware of the major damage they caused. They were only operating from the level of what they learned. So right now let's forgive them so we can really move on with our lives.

Forgiveness is never about "them"—it's always

about you! Why? Because it sets *you* free. The strength of your immune system is in direct correlation with your ability to forgive and move on. One writer so eloquently penned, "One moment of true forgiveness can erase a lifetime of guilt and fear." Let it go and grow, forgive and live.

You are the programmer now and it is up to you what you will allow to become a part of your bio-computer. At any moment you can decide what you will hold on to and what you will let go of.

Whatever you give your attention to will grow. Whatever you focus on will expand. There's a story about a wise old African chief who was approached by a young, very troubled warrior in the village. "In my head are two dogs and they are fighting all the time. One is beautiful and obedient and the other is ugly and vicious. Which one will win?" the young warrior begged. The wise chief answered, "The one you decide to feed!"

The secret to your success has a lot to do with what you will focus on. You will always move toward what you picture. Read the tabloids, watch and/or listen to dysfunctional television or radio, engage in gossip, or merely have a universal fascination with the irrelevant, and you will soon discover that the entire realm of what's possible for your life will dramatically diminish. Make it a practice to indulge in this kind of activity long enough and you will soon become a living magnet, attracting to you the people and circumstances that will rob you of the happiness, joy, and peace you so rightly deserve.

It is very important that you dwell upon the details of what you wish to achieve. Remember: What you dwell on, you dwell in. If you wish to be a singer, a musician, or a speaker, imagine yourself actually on stage performing. Go over again and again in your mind the song, the music, and the words of your speech. Feel the heat of the spotlight, the thundering sound of applause. You will always perform in a manner that is consistent with how you see yourself. Live in your imagination the experience you desire.

Before my wife and I purchased our first home, we thought of ourselves occupying it, walking from room to room, sitting in the home theatre enjoying a movie, eating in the dining room, and sleeping in the bedroom. If you desire a certain sum of money, imagine yourself counting it out; think of the rustle of the bills, feel them moving through your fingers. As these wonderful thoughts come to you, continue to frame them mentally into words, and speak them daily. **Thoughts take form.** Repeat this! Knowing and understanding this awesome principle—you can be more specific and detailed.

Arthur L. Andrews

Smile as you think. Recent studies reveal that the mere act of smiling produces a feeling of pleasure. So smile. Experience a sense of pleasure as you think about the achievement of your desire. Dr. Charles Garfield, a Berkeley research psychologist who wrote *Peak Performance* and helped train the first astronauts discovered that, "Great accomplishments are always the result of imagination. Almost all world-class athletes, astronauts, and other peak performers are visualizers. They see it, feel it, and experience it before they do it."

No one has ever better demonstrated the power of this principle than world-renowned visionary, Walt Disney. He often took his daughters to a local park to ride the merry-go-round and play. While sitting on a bench eating snacks and watching his children enjoy their rides on the carousel, Disney imagined an elaborate family park filled with happy families. He put every detail into place. From the Pirates of the Caribbean to Main Street USA, Disneyland is the result of Disney's ability to create the future in his mind. This pioneer of family amusement had no similar facilities to draw from. He relied on his imagination to design the original blueprint.

Napoleon Hill wrote, "Just as the oak tree develops from the germ that lies in the acorn, and the bird develops from the germ that lies asleep in the egg, so will your material achievement grow out of the organized plans that you create in your imagination. First comes the thought; then organization of that thought into ideas and plans; then transformation of those plans into reality. The beginning, as you will observe, is in your imagination."

Power Method: Write the *vision*. This is a detailed description of what you want, exactly as you desire to have it.   This is important because when you write, the physical movements of your fingers, hand, wrist, and forearm convey a powerful message to your subconscious.   Make up your mind that you really desire what you are writing about. Read it three times daily: morning, noon, and night. There is no need to make this some boring, mysterious ritual; simply go over the words slowly and thoughtfully.   Get some privacy and read it out loud! Do you really want this?

Action Point

Take a moment and think about what you really want in life. Think it through carefully. Visualize it and everything that goes with it.

The reason I ask this question is because most people often think they want something without realizing what it involves. You may want to go into business for yourself, but are you willing to miss that biweekly check you are so accustomed to until you achieve the desired outcome? Are you willing to do what it takes?

Recent studies reveal that there are three major reasons that most people don't succeed in life: 1) lack of passion, 2) fear of rejection, and 3) attempting too much at first.

Are you passionate about this endeavor? By detailing and reviewing your vision you will find out if this is really for you. Finally, don't bite off more than you can chew! Balance is the key.

The Art of Self-Leadership
Summary
Chapter 2

Controlled, focused thought can and will change your life.

Write and define the vision as neatly as you can.

Read the statement of your desire three times daily.

Boldly and loudly declare your desire.

Think about it at all times.

Examine it with enthusiasm.

React to it with confidence.

Smile when you think about it.

Keep it to yourself.

Chapter 3

The Power Of Keeping A Secret

The Power of Keeping a Secret

"Silence cannot be quoted—it will never, ever betray you."
-Arthur L. Andrews

In previous chapters I have made reference to the importance of secrecy and why not to talk about your core desires and plans. In order to achieve massive results you must maintain this law strictly throughout this personal development program.

There are, unfortunately, many people who are so negative and toxic that if they went into a darkroom they'll develop. A writer once said that these people need to wear a sign that reads, "Prolonged exposure causes damage." If you are planning a parade, they'll rain on it. So if you don't want them to rain on it, don't let them know which street it's coming down.

In the early nineties I was sick and tired of being sick and tired, doing just enough not to get fired, paid enough not to quit, and just hanging in there for the dental plan. After exhaustive research, Deepak Chopra and a group of Boston Behavioral scientists discovered that more people die Monday morning than any other day of the week. They discovered that the number one risk of heart disease is job dissatisfaction—doing something that does not give them a sense of meaning and fulfillment.

I made up my mind that I would live my life in celebration rather than desperation. You know there's a Chinese proverb that says, "When the student is ready the teacher appears."

I believe that is why you were led to pick up this book, because you're ready to take your life to the next level. Am I right or am I right? Well, I did what you are doing right now. I made a decision to immerse myself in a process of ongoing personal development. An internationally-known motivational speaker and now personal friend, Les Brown, inspired me. After watching one of his videos, I said to myself, "I can do that!" When I found out what he earned I said, "God is able!"

I got excited and told my wife that God spoke to me and that the spirit of determination was on me, and I felt He was telling me to quit my job. She said, "Wrong spirit! Arthur that is not the spirit of determination; that is the spirit of unemployment."

I told one of my aunts about what I was preparing to do and she responded with, "How are you going to eat?" Some of your family and friends, perhaps with the best intentions, may try to divert you from your planned course of action, but hold your course anyway. If you announce your plans to lose weight at the annual family Thanksgiving dinner they may say, "Haven't we heard that before? Weren't you on that Atkins thing? Now look at you, you gained it all back. We told you last year it wouldn't work, didn't we? Now can we enjoy this meal and would you please pass the sweet potatoes?"

When people can't see for themselves, they can't see it for you! If they know about your plans to become financially independent by starting your new enterprise, you may hear things like, "You know most businesses fail in the first six months.

Are you sure you're willing to lose everything you've worked for? Your job may not be the greatest but at least you've got security." Take it from me— it's not worth the risk!

If they know you are planning to further your education you may hear, "Do you know how old you are? Do you know how old you will be by the time you graduate?" My sister tried that and her husband almost drove her crazy!

You could build a strong case for your argument but why waste precious time and emotional energy trying to convince someone who doesn't share your consciousness anyway? Remember: "A person convinced against their will is of the same opinion still." Tell the world what you're going to do, but show it first.

If you talk about your plans, some people who hear you will be too kind or courteous to say anything discouraging to your face, but may have a lot of critical or pessimistic things to say behind your back:

"He needs his head examined, putting us through this!"

"You know what's going to happen, as soon as the yogurt hits the fan; he'll be up in our faces asking for a loan."

"You can't teach some people certain things so I guess he'll have to learn the hard way."

Even if they don't undermine you verbally, they are likely to think in terms of your failure. They will hold those thoughts in their minds, turn them over again and again, and be on the lookout to see if their gloomy, negative, and toxic predictions are being fulfilled. The atmosphere of behind-the-back criticism and toxic thought can be extremely damaging to your dreams. It has been said, "Many a dream has died Arthur, because it was shared with the wrong person."

Some of the members of the "discouragement club" are people who are closest to you. Their close connection with you and intimate knowledge of you gives their thoughts extra power to hinder you. Therefore it is very important that you keep your dreams, ideas, and concepts from those who are close to you. Don't resist this teach point; it will spare you a lot of heartache and grief. I know this from personal experience, so trust me.

The act of talking about your desired outcome or dream leaks your creative power. Some refer to this as psychic steam. There is a force of creative thought-power that you build up as you work on your dream, and this power can be drained when you are constantly moving your lips.

Creative people use this dynamic thought-power to build momentum. Read the inspirational stories of artists, leaders, inventors, and musicians. They usually don't talk about unfinished works. Most painters will not show unfinished pictures; most authors will not allow you to read partial manuscripts or discuss unwritten ideas. Avoid criticism and opposition from outside forces while strengthening your creative power by embracing the power of secrecy.

Even after you have achieved the desired results don't talk about them! Wallace Wattles gives some awesome counsel from his book *The Science of*

Getting Rich. He writes, "Do not **boast** or **brag** of your success or talk about it unnecessarily; true faith is never boastful. Wherever you find a boastful person, you find one who is secretly doubtful and afraid."

Bragging comes from insecurity and scarcity, which in essence stems from low self-esteem. It says, "I'm needy; I need acknowledgement and approval from others to feel complete." Seeking praise, trying to be noticed through sharing information that you think will make you look and feel important will only weaken you. It will destroy your true power, and the stress it will produce can and will make you sick.

Want to be respected and honored? Respect and honor yourself! Want to be accepted? Accept yourself! Want to be acknowledged and recognized? Acknowledge and recognize yourself!

Action Point

Repeat these sentences with a sense of power, conviction and renewed optimism: **I am Creative. I am Dynamic. I am Powerful. I am Productive. And I am Prosperous!** Raise your voice this time and really, really mean what you are saying! Get some privacy if you must, but just do it!

The Art of Self-Leadership

The good news is that you will reach a stage in your experience where your life, character, and circumstances are improving noticeably. Someone may ask, "What are you doing?" Don't start the self-praise and progress report. Just say, **"I am working on myself, improving my performance, and taking advantage of opportunities."** If the inquirer persists in endeavoring to get more information, give him/her the name of this book and the website and then let them draw their own conclusions.

There is one exception to the rule of keeping a secret. This is it: There will be instances in your life when sharing an idea with the right person can be advantageous to you and your dream. Notice I emphasize *"the right person!"* When I am preparing a keynote speech or training, I discuss it with a proven, trusted friend and coach. Why? Because his aim is my aim. He will not criticize or obstruct me. He will not hamper me with negative thoughts.

In a situation like this you will not leak away your creative power by discussing a project. Discussion with a creatively- and alive-thinking human being stimulates a greater flow of helpful ideas than either partner could produce alone, or than two could produce separately, so choose your associate(s) carefully and prayerfully!

Remember that critics and snipers will try to tear

you down even if you have succeeded at something. Maybe that's why the world's greatest teacher was aware of this danger. Several times after healing people He warned them not to say anything about it!

The danger is clear. Skeptics would say to the newly-healed person, "Oh, I hope you know this so-called healing is only temporary; give it a few weeks and it will probably get worse."

We can truly learn a lesson about keeping our mouths shut by observing the oyster. "When the moon is full the oyster opens completely. When the crab sees one it throws a piece of stone or seaweed into it and the oyster cannot close again so that it serves the crab for meat. Such is the fate of the person who opens his or her mouth too much and thereby puts themselves at the mercy of the listener."-Leonardo da Vinci

The Art of Self-Leadership
Summary
Chapter 3

Secrecy accelerates your accomplishments.

Secrecy helps you avoid criticism and sarcasm.

Secrecy helps you escape well-intentioned meddling.

Secrecy helps you escape negative thought poison.

Secrecy helps you conserve rich-prosperous ideas.

Don't toot your own horn.

Give no detailed description of your plans.

Choose your associate(s) carefully and prayerfully.

Chapter 4

The Power Of Words

The Power of Words

"The right word spoken at the right time is a
powerful agent."
-Arthur L. Andrews

Speech and thought are like Siamese twins; they are
intimately connected. Unfortunately, you and I
have paid the high price of speaking before thinking. What you say shapes your destiny. From time
to time you find yourself in situations where your
outcome depends largely on your ability to communicate effectively: preparing for an interview,
meeting new people, delivering a speech, making a
sales presentation, and dealing with family, friends,
or coworkers.

Marshall Sylver had it right when he said, "To get
what you want you must communicate with others
in a way that inspires them to give it to you."

An inappropriate word can shatter a meaningful
relationship. However, the right words spoken at
the right time can win over your adversary. An
indiscreet remark or a loud angry outburst can

destroy your credibility. What comes out of your mouth really makes a difference in the way you are perceived and treated by others.

Clifford seizes every opportunity of telling how he lost his job through the personal spite of his lousy boss. He has a great dramatic gift and repeats the story flawlessly to his friends or whoever meets him in the street that makes the fatal mistake of asking, "How are things going?"

He tells his story to the people at the employment agency. He tells it to prospective employers when he goes looking for work. He has written letters to the paper exposing the injustice of it all and has aired his grievance on a hot-line radio talk show. He has developed a reputation as a chronic whiner and wonders why he can't seem to find employment.

Clifford has a real grievance, for sure. Yet he is not alone in that. We all have had our share of heartaches, and the truth of the matter is that eighty-percent of the people listening to you really don't care about your stuff and the other twenty-percent are relieved it's happening to you and not them.

Chronic complaining alienates your family and friends, but what's worse is that it will have an adverse effect on you if you don't stop it. What you keep negatively bringing up in conversation will eventually bring you down.

Be more conscious of what comes out of your mouth. Stop talking about negative, toxic, and unpleasant topics. If someone you know is having a difficult experience, don't run around telling everyone. Don't be so quick to talk about the cat that died, the car that got repossessed, the house that burned to the ground, or the meteorite that fell and wiped out an entire golf course. If any of these things really disturb you—and if you can do something about it by your thoughts, speech, deeds, money, or vote—then stand up, face it, and take action! But don't worry or grieve or talk about things you cannot correct. Save your emotional, physical, and vocal dynamics for things that are within your power.

Don't talk too much. Excessive talking does nobody any good. It depletes your reservoir of vital energy. It does not fortify your mind or anyone else's. Most people talk too much, and what they have to say is often just a lot of empty sentences designed to keep them entertained. Now this does not mean that you must avoid talking; just choose your words carefully and prayerfully.

A creative, dynamic, powerful, and productive person doesn't waste words by vacillating and drifting, but instead thinks through what he or she intends to share. They ask questions like, "Is it true?

Is it kind? And is it necessary?" Review your output of words.

A famous anonymous author said, "A sharp tongue and a brilliant mind are never found in the same skull." The wrong choice of words can make your life miserable.

During the air traffic controller's strike, a passenger watched a negative, toxic executive demean and belittle a baggage handler who wasn't moving fast enough for him. When the passenger endeavored to empathize with the young man for having to put up with such abuse and lack of respect, the baggage handler assured the passenger that he was okay and everything would be all right— he had already received his just reward. After a brief moment of silence the passenger asked, "What do you mean?" The baggage handler replied with a huge smile on his face, "He's going to New York, but his bags are going to London."

The Book of Life says, "Whatever you sow, that must you also reap" (Galatians 6:7). So it is with words. Whatever you say will produce a corresponding return. Talk about things you want to experience. Talk about great health, wealth, and prosperity. You can do this without violating your commitment to secrecy.

Keep talking this way and you will start thinking

this way. Remain true to *your* visions, *your* dreams, and *your* values, and your life will shine.

Power Quote: "What you speak about, you think about. What you think about, you bring about!"

Action Point

Say this again and again. What I speak about, I think about. *It will work when you work it.*

Power Method: Monitor your conversation for the next hour and think about what you are about to say before you speak. If it's not positive or uplifting to the hearer don't speak it. At first, try this exercise once or twice a week. You will find it easy. You can then extend your monitoring until all your conversation becomes constructive and positive.

Make praise a part of your mental diet. Make it a habit to share sincere compliments, thanks, and appreciative words, whenever and wherever you can. The habit of giving praise is a great aid in winning and maintaining friendship and love.

Mary Kay Ash, founder of Mary Kay Cosmetics, said, "No matter how busy you are, you must take time to make the other person feel important."

Motivational speaker Dennis Kimbro tells an awesome story about an executive who arrived at his office a few hours earlier than usual. No one was there when he arrived except George, the custodian. George was a faithful employee with many years of service to the company. When his boss walked into the office, George was emptying trashcans, dusting furniture, and cleaning the office. When George's boss noticed him doing his daily routine, he said, "George, you know, as I look around the building I can't help thinking what an asset you've been to our organization. You've always kept this place clean and tidy. George, you're an important part of our team, and I want you to know that I appreciate you and all that you have done."

George paused then replied, "Thank you sir," and walked out of the room with his dust cloth in hand. A few minutes passed. Suddenly the office door opened, and in walked George. His eyes were moist; there was a tear on his cheek. His boss didn't understand. He said, "What's wrong? Did I say something to offend you?"

George forced a smile and then replied, "No sir, you didn't offend me. But I have something I would like to share with you. I've worked for this company for twenty years, and this morning is the first time anyone has ever told me that they appreciated anything I've ever done." He continued, "I just want you to know that I appreciate what you said more than I've ever appreciated my paycheck!" Someone once said, "The deepest craving in human nature is the desire to be appreciated."

An IBM executive put it this way, "You can foul up on almost anything, and you'll get another chance. But if you screw up, even a little bit, on people management, you're gone. That's it, top performer or not." Wow, what a statement!

A married couple went on vacation, and the husband decided it was time to teach the wife how to play tennis. By the third day the wife picked up the tennis racket, looked at her husband and said, "Okay, today tell me what I'm doing right." Remember: People perform better under praise rather than criticism.

Power Method: Start practicing right now to find something pleasant to say to every person you meet. Try it on cashiers, coworkers, your mother-in-law, the IRS agent, at the next family reunion, the postal worker standing behind the counter, or at the next church board meeting. Seek out something that you can sincerely praise them for wearing or doing.

For example:

"I look forward to seeing that beautiful smile on your face; it's so encouraging."

"Wow, you're moving this morning. You must be full of energy, and I like that!"

"You are always on time! That says a lot about your integrity!"

[Action Point]

Find someone in your work environment or home and share this powerful phrase with him or her: You are really looking (good/strong/happy/energetic/peaceful/confident...) today.

Don't stop there. Praise the person behind their back. This is the most gracious compliment of all. And be sure of this one thing—it will get back to them. Speak to and treat others the way you would have them speak to and treat you.

There will be some who may resent your powerful, positive disposition. Be positive anyway! Remember: "All the water in the world cannot drown you unless you let it get inside your boat."

The Art of Self-Leadership

Summary
Chapter 4

Your conversation shapes your life.

What you say and how you say it determines other people's perception of you.

Change your thoughts and change your mind.

Talk about what you want to experience.

Don't talk too much.

Speak positively about other people.

Don't share your troubles.

Praise people.

Chapter 5

The Power Of Can

The Power of Can

"Good timber doesn't grow with ease; the stronger
the wind the stronger the trees."
J.W. Marriott

Where there's a will, there is a way. Every time you
overcome one obstacle in your life, you gain more
power, more creativity, and more self-confidence to
face the next challenge. I believe it would be mis-
leading to suggest that this system or any other will
lead you to achieve all your desires without any
interference or setbacks. Never stop moving toward
your goal because of opposition or because you
made a mistake.

The difference between people who are successful
and people who are not is the amount of time it
takes for them to get over a major disappointment.
It's their uncanny ability to rise up from the canvas
of life when unforeseen circumstances knock them
down.

EVERYBODY MAKES MISTAKES

Arthur L. Andrews

I believe the famous author anonymous had it right again when he or she wrote, *"Mistakes are the portals of discovery."* The piano student plays tens of thousands of wrong notes before he is fit to perform the simplest piece in public. But the student does not quit at the first wrong note, or the hundredth, or the thousandth. The teacher shows the student that, in learning to detect wrong notes, he is training his ear to produce the right ones.

The beginning skater's ankles are too weak to support her weight. Her sense of balance is untrained. She falls repeatedly. By wobbling and tumbling she learns what not to do, and in time can move gracefully on her skates.

The aspiring speaker trembles and turns pale as he faces his first audience. His voice is weak and shrill; he forgets half of what he meant to say. He finally sits down, drenched in sweat, convinced he has made an eternal fool of himself. But he rises again, speaks again, corrects his errors, and today is an internationally known Empowerment Specialist. (I bet you can't guess whom I'm talking about.)

By now I'm sure you get the point. A setback is nothing but a set up for a comeback.

The Art of Self-Leadership

Action Point

Right now stop reading and say these words: "YES I CAN AND YES I WILL!" Say it again and again!

Set aside some time to read the biographies of successful men and women who succeeded against all odds in achieving their dreams. You will find that all of them made mistakes, and endured opposition and hardships as well as setbacks.

Nelson Mandela spent twenty-seven years of his adult life in prison for his dream of destroying apartheid. His life was one of waiting and winning. When he was finally released from prison he screamed out "Amandla!"—the Xhosa term for *power*. The people knew he was the man for the job, and to international acclaim was inducted as president of South Africa May 9, 1994.

Mary Tyler Moore had it right when she said, "Pain nourishes courage. You can't be brave if you've only had wonderful things happen to you."

Keep this thought in mind that wherever you are, whatever your circumstances may be, whatever misfortune you may have suffered, the final chapter to your life has not been written yet. There's still time left on the clock, so get back in the game of life and score!

As an elementary student actor, James Earl Jones stuttered so badly he communicated with friends and teachers using written notes. He didn't let that stop him. Today James Earl Jones is in demand as a voiceover personality for the richness and power of his voice.

Remember: Circumstances can only strip the music from your life if you allow them to. Many years ago, a young man succeeded in splitting the bull's eye on the target again and again at the Olympics. His eye-hand coordination won him a gold medal. Then adversity struck. He lost his right shooting arm. Four years later he returned to the games and split the bull's eye as he had done before, this time using his left hand.

Homer said, "Adversity has a way of eliciting talents which in prosperous circumstances would have lain dormant." Life is like a grindstone; whether it polishes you or grinds you down depends on your attitude.

Sometimes your plan or program will succeed promptly and easily. You immediately get the information you requested, the position, the creative idea, or the assistance you've needed for so long. But often you will meet opposition and setbacks. The relationship that has kept you going suddenly dissolves; the grant is denied; the prospective buyer decides to go with another vendor; your teenager announces that you are going to be a grandparent; your test comes back positive; your services are no longer required by your employer; you fall off your diet; and the list goes on ....

This is a testing time—a period that separates the winners from the losers. There are three common reactions to adversity, criticism, delays, disappointments, failures, and opposition:

1) Putting self down. "I should have known that they would not give me the position! Every time it looks like I'm about to get ahead or make an extra amount of money, I blow it!!! I'm just not a good talker. I should have never stuck my neck out there like that. I feel so stupid!" As a man thinketh so is he!

2) Blaming other people. "They are just jealous of me! They don't know a good thing when they see it. If my parents were there for me I could have at least had a fighting chance. I know now why I wasn't elected—so and so had been talking about me. You made me do it! You make me sick!" No one can make you sick. It's the sick thoughts about them that are making you sick. Stop the blame game and assume responsibility for your life.

3) **Being stubborn and refusing to change.** "I know this is the right way; God gave me this plan and I will not compromise the integrity of it. You're all wrong and I refuse to listen to this nonsense. I've spent too much time on this just to have you reject it! No!!!"

Remember: "Progress and growth are impossible if we do things the way we've always done things." Maybe, it's time to change?

Power Method: There is a much easier and more constructive way to face a setback.

1. See what you can learn from the setback. Don't get discouraged. Manage your emotions. Keep calm, poised, and confident, and ask a few questions:

   Did I properly and thoroughly prepare?
   Did I follow through?
   Did I overlook something?
   Did I fall short?
   Why did they oppose my idea?

2. Take full responsibility for mistakes, apologize for errors, laugh at yourself, and admit when you need help. Bounce back from a setback by telling yourself: "Look, I didn't do my best, and I was properly ill-prepared,"

or "Even if I was superbly prepared, well, that's life and everyone has the right to choose," or "It maybe my time but just not my turn!" or "God's delays are not his denials!" When in doubt, ask. When I experience rejection for any reason, I always inquire as to what was it that kept me from securing this opportunity. This affords me the chance to upgrade my skills and better prepare myself to meet the next challenge.

3. Study to improve! Many years ago Earl Nightingale said that one hour per day of study in your chosen field is all it takes. One hour per day of study will put you at the top of your field within three years. Within five years you'll be a national authority. In seven years, you can be one of the best people in the world at what you do.

4. Say great things to a great person ... you! Your assignment is to read the following affirmations daily: I am happy and successful! I can make it! I am creative, dynamic, and healthy! I am unstoppable! I always bounce back! I am courageous! I give more than I take! I am learning new things every day! I welcome challenge! I am a success! I am present and ready to act!

5. Relax! Maintain your composure.

Sir Winston Churchill and Lady Astor had one of the more bitter relationships recorded in history. They constantly insulted each other, both continually adding fuel to the fire. On one occasion Lady Astor was upset over a decision that went in favor of the renowned politician. She yelled at him, saying, "Sir Winston, if you were my husband I'd poison your tea." Churchill fired back, "And if you were my wife I'd be happy to drink it!"

Very often when people suffer setbacks they have a tendency to lash out at others for no apparent reason. Blaming or speaking negative, toxic, spirit-destroying words are not the way to effectively deal with disappointments or setbacks; they only make matters worse.

Action Point

Ask yourself this question: Am I blaming someone else for my disappointments or failures? If the answer is "yes," then forgive and move on today!

Happy and successful people succeed in spite of difficulties, not in the absence of difficulties. While losers are looking for someone to blame, winners are looking for solutions.

I love what George Bernard Shaw said about the

blame game:

"People are always blaming their circumstances for what they are. I don't believe in circumstances. The people who get on in this world are the people who get up and look for the circumstances they want, and if they can't find them, make them."

Happy, successful people take full responsibility for what's going on in their lives. For example, if you are blaming your parents for giving you a bad start in life, decide right now that it is up to you to do something about it. If you are blaming the lousy English professor for you not getting the editorial position, take responsibility. If your family is dysfunctional, it is up to you to stay functional and happy.

When you suffer a setback or experience disappointment, it's a big wake up call. It's a signal to change. It is your personal invitation to do something different—not more of the same! After all, you already know the definition for insanity: doing the same thing over and over again and expecting a different outcome.

When I was a little boy riding my bicycle in the streets of Brooklyn, New York, every now and then I would experience what we referred to as a slow leak in one of my tires. Ever had one? Rather than repair the tire I would go to the local gas station and get more air, and ride until I needed more. The answer to my dilemma was not more air; the answer was to find the leak and plug it.

Your challenge is to find and plug any leaks in your system. As you face and plug each hole, you will begin to turn every challenge into a gift.

Action Point

Take an objective look at your resume, business plan, or presentation. Ask yourself, "Is this worthy of being labeled "first class" or is it less than my very best?"

I recall when my phone wasn't ringing, and no one was booking me for speaking engagements. I used to become so discouraged that I actually entertained the thoughts of giving up speaking altogether. I was so tired of the rejections and cancellations that I didn't want to pick up the phone and dial anymore for fear of rejection. It was easier for me to blame, whine, and make excuses for my failures, than to take the necessary action to create opportunities for myself.

One consequence of whining is that it manifests in statements like: "The problem with them is they don't know a good thing when they see it," or

"After all these years why hasn't anyone discovered my talents?" and "Trying to earn a living shouldn't be this hard."

The objective approach is to understand that life is like a huge Wal-Mart, with many products to choose from. Your challenge is to provide uniqueness and value to people. Remember: "If they can't get it anywhere else, you determine the price."

Earl Nightingale, the dean of motivational speakers, put it this way: "The amount of money that you receive will always be in direct ratio to the demand for what you do, your ability to do it, and the difficulty in replacing you." If you represent excellence and uniqueness, you will be in demand with clients, employers, and friends, as well as family. If not, you will get left on the shelf.

As a speaker, I have met numerous struggling speakers who blame their audiences, the economy, and everybody but themselves for their lack of success. They say things like, "I don't know what's wrong with these audiences; they're so boring and dead!" or "They don't seem to value great speaking," or "Do they know who I am?" or "I am an orator; they should pay me!"

That's foolishness! Why should I pay you if I didn't enjoy your speech? My good friend and coach, Walter G. Ballard, listened to my ranting one time when I had given probably one of the worst speeches of my life. I felt abandoned because people were fleeing. I tried to rationalize that I was suffering persecution because they were probably jealous and couldn't handle the truth. He looked me straight in the eyes and told *me* the truth, "Arthur you were not prepared!"

Walter risked our friendship to tell me what I needed to hear, not what I wanted to hear. Allan Cohen was right when he said, "We must welcome people into our lives that require more of us than we do of ourselves." Very often the disappointment, setbacks, or even rejections that we experience are sometimes the direct result of inadequate preparation.

Remember, the best way to predict your future is to create it! Yes you can, and yes you will!

The Art of Self-Leadership
Summary
Chapter 5

Where there's a will, there's a way.

Everybody makes mistakes.

Yes I can and yes I will.

Pain nourishes courage.

Stop the blame game.

Learn from your setbacks.

Take full responsibility for your life.

Find the hole in your system and plug it.

Read affirmations daily.

Chapter 6

The Power Of Ask

The Power of Ask

I once read that asking for something increases the likelihood of getting it. The first time I read that it didn't mean much, but the more I thought about it and related it to real life, the more truth I saw in it. In fact, I now truly believe it's a law— a spiritual law that says, "When you ask, you receive."

This law will work if you work it! It will work for you no matter what field you are in. Recent studies reveal that the most natural and most effective method ever devised for closing the sale is simply to ask for the order. Salespeople have actually revealed that their sales have skyrocketed when they began to do one simple thing: ASK FOR THE ORDER!

Here we see that many salespeople limit themselves and don't make sales because they simply don't ask. They don't ASK FOR THE ORDER!

This same principle carries over into the other areas of our lives. Often we only enjoy a fraction of our potential because we don't ask for more. Life will pay you what you think you're worth and what you ask for. If you are providing a service, it is extremely important that you receive what you think you are worth, be it in cash or whatever channel is of value to you. Most people are not clear on the true value of their services and that is why they don't know what to ask for. They're hoping that the recipient will recognize their worth and reward them accordingly. It doesn't work like that in the real world. **You** must determine the true value of your services in fee or exchange and ASK FOR IT! *When you honor what you do, others will also.*

Offer your work only to those who value it. If you work for a company or organization that doesn't value your contribution, it eventually decreases your level of self-confidence.

I reduced my fee for years thinking I would get more speaking appointments. The first thing I experienced was a feeling of resentment for allowing myself to be paid less than I felt I was worth. That's not a good feeling! But who's to blame for this? Surely it wasn't the clients; they just simply paid the invoice. Second, I was subconsciously accepting the fact that speaking wasn't worth that much, and guess what? I stopped getting phone calls! Profound, isn't it?

It's also true in the world of dating. In my travels I

have tremendous opportunities to meet people from all walks of life. I've talked to many young men who wanted to know how they could get girls to go out with them. So often the challenge was that they didn't get dates because of their fear of rejection.

I heard a story the other day about a guy who finally met the woman of his dreams. She was everything he ever wanted in a woman. This girl was extremely beautiful and intelligent. She was so charismatic that every time he was about to speak he was at a loss for words. He wanted badly to date her, but his "negative chatter box" kept suggesting that he was not good enough, and he allowed this to hold him back.

What if he asked her out and she turned him down? He'd be so embarrassed and humiliated!

To play it safe, he became friends with her. He'd call her on the phone from time to time and they would go to work-related functions. This young man reasoned that at least this platonic relationship placed him in a comfort zone. He got to enjoy the company of this beautiful woman and not have to deal with the pain of rejection if his request to build something more serious was declined. But this wasn't what he wanted!

Finally, after months of rehearsing different scenarios in his mind, he could stand it no longer. He mustered up the courage to tell her that he was interested in her and wanted to take her out on a real date. To his surprise she accepted and he was euphoric! He was extremely nervous and self-conscious. He showed up at her door. She looked fantastic! She put her arms around him and he began to shake uncontrollably. Beads of perspiration started to pop on his forehead. For some strange reason he was losing his composure.

Did you know that fear has a way of showing up in our physiology? She didn't utter a word in regard to his behavior, but rather tactfully shifted his attention to a book that she gently placed in his hands. He thanked her and proceeded to escort her to his car where he set the book in a compartment next to him. The first stop was to see a hilarious comedic play in which they both thoroughly enjoyed themselves. Next, they went to dinner. Everything was going well until he started feeling anxious and nervous about their future. He thought to himself, "Does she really like me or is she just being cordial?" and "Will she accept another invitation to go out?" and "Does she have somebody on the side that she's not telling me about?" and "I don't want to get hurt again," and "Maybe it's best that we remain as friends."

His fearful thoughts about the future kept him from being fully-present and enjoying the company of this beautiful and charming woman. Suddenly the rest of the evening became a chore. His date constantly inquired if everything was all right and was it something she did or said. "What happened?" she'd ask. "It seems that you shut down all of a sudden. Is it that you are not feeling well?"

Unfortunately, he allowed his poor self-image to affect his chances of ever going out with her again. At the end of the evening the two sat in silence as he drove her back to her place. She politely said good night and he went home feeling dejected. He knew that he had blown it. He was so depressed and embarrassed that he decided not to call her again.

A year after their date he heard through the grapevine that she was getting married. All of his negative questions and thoughts had become his concrete reality.

More than a decade passed. By this time he had had a series of relationships but none could measure up to the vision of what could have been had he not been so insecure about himself.

One day he received a call from his best friend. His friend soberly reported that the woman he had pined over for so long had died of breast cancer. The funeral was to take place on Wednesday. His friend reminded him that he still had a book in his library that was loaned to him years ago—the same one that this woman gave the young man on that fateful first date.

"Did you ever read the book?" his friend asked. He continued, "Hey man, on the inside cover there was a note she wrote to you."

"Read it to me," said the young man. "What does it say?"

The friend opened the note and read, "It's tonight or never."

She would have jumped a tall building in a single bound just to be with him but he never knew it. Someone once wrote, "Missed opportunities are the curse of potential."

This story must have hit you like a ton of caffeine! I know you're probably thinking about the numerous times in your life when you dreaded to **ASK!** There were times when you *coulda, shoulda, woulda,* but didn't!

Just think of all the times you were robbed of things you could have had—if you had only *asked.* Let's not let history repeat itself ever again!

There are at least four principles I want you to embrace right now: **DESIRE, BELIEF,**

DETERMINATION, and PERSISTENCE.

These four things go together to make up faith. When you mix faith with your asking, you'll receive. Remember: "If you entertain fear, it will interfere with your faith."

In Matthew 7:7-8, the Book of Life admonishes us: "Keep on asking and it will be given you; keep on seeking and you will find; keep on knocking and the door will be opened to you: For everyone who keeps on asking receives; and he who keeps on seeking finds; and to him who keeps on knocking, the door will be opened."

I believe that sufficient faith, or belief, makes anything possible. It motivates us to action. Many of our limitations are caused by a lack of faith, lack of belief, and lack of asking. Asking involves action.

The greatest teacher I believe to have walked this planet said, "You have not because you ask not!" Lack of faith causes you not to ask. There's no motivation to action when there's no belief. But with belief, all things are possible.

Wow! Just think of it! You can get anything, *anything,* if you ask in prayer and believe (Mark 11). Then make a plan and go after it!

Write down the three things that you fear are keeping you back. Then ask yourself—*Why am I afraid of these?*

Desire is the starting point of all successful endeavors. Unless you have a desire, you will never get started. ***Discouragement will never overwhelm me when my desire to succeed is strong enough.***

It is *so* important that you comprehend this powerful principle that I am going to ask you to repeat these words below. As you repeat these words, recall an experience where a strong desire caused you to overcome your fear of asking. ***"Discouragement will never overwhelm me when my desire to succeed is strong enough."***

Think back in your life when you overcame the fear of asking because your desire was so strong. Stop reading and think for a moment. What just popped into your mind?

One experience that pops into my mind goes way back to when I was a little boy and had a strong desire to sing. There were members of my family and people who I saw in the church community who were very gifted in this talent. I was timid and shy in those days.

One day I decided to face my fear and sang in front of my church community. It was a nerve-shattering experience, to say the least! I panned the room and almost fainted. I started to cry and even lost control of one of my bodily functions. My peers were cracking up with laughter. They clowned me for months. Even so-called "loved ones" weren't all that comforting. Sometimes people don't have to say a single thing; all they have to do is look a certain way when you make a request. Sometimes you decide that it's safer not to ask. It took me almost twenty years before I asked to sing again.

I was living in Huntsville, Alabama and struggling trying to make it as a motivational speaker. One day I was sitting around, eating Doritos and feeling sorry for myself. I started thumbing through the local newspaper and I noticed an ad that read: Auditioning for singers to sing the National Anthem for the local basketball team. I hesitated for a moment. "What if I don't get it and look like a fool?" I immediately flipped the script and challenged that "negative chatterbox" with, "What if I *do* get it?

Do you remember me telling you that we always perform in a manner that is consistent with how we see ourselves? I am not going to tell you that I was not afraid, but I was also afraid not to. I made the necessary call, spoke to the coordinator, set up the appointment, and showed up. Eighty-five percent of success is showing up. There were other singers who had more talent and experience but I didn't let that stop me.

When they called my name I didn't move for fifteen seconds and they had to call me again: "Mr. Arthur L. Andrews, will you please come to center stage to give your rendition of the National Anthem."

I stood there frozen with fear, rehearsing negative experiences of my past rather than painting a positive image on the canvas of my imagination. The audition was not impressive at all. I sang in a key that was too high for me and ended up sounding like the character Alfalfa from "The Little Rascals."

They stopped me before I was finished and thanked me for my energy. My energy? What? I was embarrassed, humiliated, and scared to go home because I had announced that I was going to nail this thing! (Me and my big mouth!) As I was gathering my articles to depart, a voice so strong inside was telling me to stop, turn around, and ask for another chance. I'm thinking to myself, "Am I a pain seeker?" Again the voice said, "ASK TO SING AGAIN." By this time I was thinking to myself, "What do I have to lose?"

I learned something about belief; there are basically two types: emotional and intellectual.

Intellectual belief is to know something because you've studied it, read it, or been told about it. Emotional belief is to know something because you've experienced it. There's a world of difference. Think about that for a moment! [Back to the story.]

I started to engage in some power talk: "The mark of greatness is truly upon me and I must not be limited by the shortsighted belief of others. I can because I think I can. I can because God says I can. I'm looking good. I'm feeling good. I smell good! I'm an awesome, creative, dynamic expression of life. And I got it goin' on!"

I shouted across the massive arena, "I want another shot at this!" They acted as if they didn't hear me, so I repeated it as if I never said it before, "I want to get another shot at it!"

Someone replied, "Mr. Andrews, you had your opportunity." I said again, "I want another one! Are you denying me the opportunity to have another chance at displaying my genius and creativity in *historic* Alabama?" For some strange reason this got their attention and they allowed me to audition again. They gave me the chance I needed—a second one.

This time I was determined and focused. I told them I would do it a cappella. After all, that is how

I rehearsed at home. I was now entering the zone of emotional belief: a cool, objective kind of belief. It's a motivator. It causes you to say to yourself, "I know I can do this; I have never done it at this level before but I'm sure I can do it! I have rehearsed and I am prepared! Let's do this!" I got behind that microphone, visualized my success, sang powerfully and watched them reverse their decision about me. **YES!!!**

Desire isn't always equated with huge self-confidence. Desire produces the persistence and determination to keep going after what it is you truly want. When you do, you're bound to experience some success, and as that happens, your enthusiasm and confidence to ask grows.

POWER QUOTE: "It's a funny thing about life—those who are willing to settle for less than the best usually get it." -W. Somerset Maugham

POWER METHOD: Ask yourself—
1. How challenging is it for you to ask things of others?
2. Why do you have this fear of asking?
3. How has this fear influenced your life?
4. What do you plan to do right now to overcome this fear?

Chapter 7

The Power Of Affirmations

The Power of Affirmations

This chapter is short, sweet, and to the point—please get this!

Now that you are immersed in an ongoing process of personal development, it's time to create a system that will enable you to consistently produce results. Remember: Consistency is the key.

One of the power methods I recommend is <u>affirmation:</u> *A verbal tool that is used to change attitudes, build confidence, and increase faith.*

> [Action Point]

I want you to repeat the following statements with a sense of conviction, power, and renewed optimism. Let us begin:

> "I acknowledge that true discipline is the ability to master my moods. I am totally responsible for my life and where I am right now in life. I know that if I want more I must become more. I am totally responsible

for my emotional, financial, social, and spiritual condition. I say nice things about others. I respect and honor others. I deserve the best; therefore, I give my best. I realize that not everyone is going to like me, so I'm not going to be discouraged by what people may say or think about me. What is important is what *I* say and think about me. I will treat others the way I would like to be treated. I will pay my bills on time, for this is a statement of my integrity. I am not a victim of any circumstance; I am more than a conqueror. I am beneath no one. I am a money magnet. I have incredible energy. My blood flow is awesome! I am healed. What I focus on will expand. I choose to focus on positive things. Positive, productive people are coming into my life. I am designed for greatness and manufactured for success. I am deliberate with my words. I think about what I say before I speak. I am excited about life. I will not give up. I will act as if nothing is going to stop me. I am unstoppable. I now release what I don't want. I create phenomenal wealth. I'm getting better and better at what I do. I wish _____ the best. Money just flows to me. I smile at others. I live in the moment. I love change. I am intelligent. I inspire others. I manage my food choices. I have an awesome spending plan. I expect good from expected and unexpected sources. I ask for what I want. I lose weight easily and effortlessly. I love to exercise. Something great is about to happen. I fire myself up. Tomorrow is not promised to me, so I must act now. I am moving closer to my dream. I drive, eat, live in, and wear the best. I have a first-class lifestyle. My life is on the up swing. I will never be denied. The mark of greatness is truly upon me."

Say this daily: morning, noon, and night, and get ready to experience living at a whole new level. I promise it will change your life in ways that will have you in awe. Remember: "What you say is what you get!"

I promised it would be short but it is also very, very powerful!

Chapter 8

The Power Of Release

The Power of Release

Nothing is more frustrating than being stuck! Stuck, as in doing something or being in a relationship that's going in a direction that limits you. What keeps most people stuck is that they are not aware that they have the ability and power to make magnificent choices. You are where you are and remain where you are because you have made a choice to stay there. You're resisting, fighting, clicking your heels three times, trying to ignore them, destroy them, forget them, put up with them, hoping, coping, pretending it's not happening, or whatever!!!

Are you afraid to let something go because you fear loss? Do you believe that something is better than nothing even if that something is killing you?

Would you believe that there are people who stay stuck in unfulfilling relationships and/or dead-end jobs rather than make a courageous choice to do what is right for them? To get rid of what you want, simply shift your focus. Remember what I told you: What you focus on expands. You give life and energy to whatever and wherever you give your attention! Stop creating what you don't want! Get serious about this!

Are you really getting what you want? If not, then why not? A young man asked me the other day, "Why am I broke, Mr. Andrews?" My reply was simply, "I don't know." Life is awesome. There is abundance all around you. There is always a way out of something. Life gets better when *you* get better, and you have the awesome ability and power to create your reality with the words you speak. So now, *you* tell me why you're broke. Get rid of any concepts that suggest that you don't deserve to be rich. To have anything, you have to create it, be it negative or positive. Remember, you get what you settle for.

I've discovered that it's not ridiculous what I ask for in life, but rather, what I'm willing to settle for. I have made a decision to live a first-class lifestyle. That's my decision; what's yours?

I know what I had to do in order to create phenomenal wealth for my family and me. When I started writing this book I had a lot of excuses, and used some really good ones, but the one thing that brought this project to completion is that I got rid of those excuses, and the results have been amazing!

The Art of Self-Leadership

The happiest people on the planet are the ones who are willing to let go of what's not working in their lives and follow their inner call. Some call this *purpose*.

It takes courage to let go—to move on. Stepping out of your comfort zone is the first step to healing. Do you remember the scene from "The Color Purple" when Whoopi Goldberg's character had reached her breaking point and courageously moved on? Well, that's what you have to make yourself do. The only person that can do that for you is *you*. You must move beyond your history in order to truly discover your destiny. Why would you cling to a drop of water when you have the ocean available to you?

Your life is calling you! What is your answer? Will you be pleased or perturbed, and/or delighted or disturbed at what the future will bring?

Without a strategy life becomes a tragedy. Do not fear what people will say or think. Some will laugh, criticize, or even try to challenge your decision to release; let go and move on. Just remember, that is a strong indicator that you're on the right track.

When people talk about you maliciously, it's the ultimate in flattery. It's an attempt of a lesser mind that can't cope or compete with you. Walk on!!!

Arthur L. Andrews

Summary
Chapter 8

Don't stay stuck in life.

Don't fear the fear of loss.

Shift your focus.

Your life is calling you.

Make a strategy.

CONCLUSION

If this offering has touched you in any way, please practice these principles daily. You are a master-piece of creation. Your presence on this planet is so vital. Know who you are! Walk in that knowing and deliver the gift! Most of all ... Live as if your life depends on it! It does!

Arthur L. Andrews

About
Arthur L. Andrews

Arthur L. Andrews is an award-winning speaker, author, trainer and success coach. Born and reared in Brooklyn, New York, Arthur is a product of urban life. He has experienced first-hand the awesome challenges of the streets. Before becoming a speaker, he served as a peace officer for the New York City Board of Education for ten years, receiving numerous awards of honor and heroism.

Arthur first received payment for speaking and training in 1990. Since 1990 he has given over 1,300 speeches with many of them being repeat performances. Arthur has dedicated his international speaking expertise to helping corporations and other organizations to shake off mediocrity and maximize their unlimited potential. His unique ability to capture and hold audiences spellbound has earned him the respect and business of companies such as Southwestern Bell, Kellogg's, State Farm Insurance, Lucent Technologies, Hewlett Packard, Air Jamaica, and The Stellar Awards. He continues to travel, sharing his message of hope.

Arthur L. Andrews lives in Sugar Land, Texas.

The Art of Self-Leadership
Thanks Ma!

Mary V. Andrews